BlackPrint

Cheat Codes for Succeeding in Corporate America as a Black Professional

BlackPrint

Cheat Codes for Succeeding in Corporate America as a Black Professional

Monique L. Thompson

www.BlackPrintSuccess.com

BlackPrint

Cheat Codes for Succeeding in Corporate America as a Black Professiona

Book Cover Design: Monique L. Thompson

Published in the United States of America

Copyright © 2025 Monique L. Thompson

ISBN-13: 979-8-9929033-4-8

www.BlackPrintSuccess.com

BlackPrint

Cheat Codes for Succeeding in Corporate America as a Black Professional

The board was never set in our favor.

The rules were never made for us.

But we don't just play the game—we

master, rewrite, and win it...on

our own terms.

~ Monique L. Thompson

BlackPrint

Cheat Codes for Succeeding in Corporate America as a Black Professional

BlackPrint

Cheat Codes for Succeeding in Corporate America as a Black Professional

Table of Contents

BlackPrint

Cheat Codes for Succeeding in Corporate America as a Black Professional

The Game I Didn't Know
I Was Playing

I have been in tech for over 35 years, navigating some of the most recognizable Fortune 500 companies—Microsoft, T-Mobile, HTC, Starbucks, F5, Amazon, and a few startups along the way.

When I started in the early '90s, Black women in tech were rare. And Black women who were technical? **Even rarer**. I didn't see many people who looked like me in the rooms where I worked.

I come from a long line of civil servants and military professionals—brilliant, hard-working people with no blueprint for corporate America. I grew up being told I was gifted, talented, and capable of anything. But there was always a caveat:

"You have to be twice as good just to be seen as 'good enough.'"

As a teenager, I dismissed that warning. Indeed, talent speaks for itself. Surely, if I do excellent work, the right people will notice.

I WAS WRONG. I quickly learned that there were two sets of rules. Scratch that—an entire game was being played, and we weren't even told the rules.

I remember working for a Fortune 500 tech company that proudly showcased me in diversity recruiting ads—my face in Ebony and other Black publications, proof that they were "investing in diversity." But while I was good enough to be their poster child, I wasn't "good enough" to be promoted.

That's when I learned a hard truth:

- **Brilliance** isn't enough.

- **Hard work** isn't enough.

- **Impact** isn't enough.

Because...I am Black.

I wrote this book because I spent decades learning lessons the hard way—through trial, error, and sheer resilience. I don't want you to have to do the same.

BlackPrint

Cheat Codes for Succeeding in Corporate America as a Black Professional

This book is the BlackPrint—a guide to navigating corporate spaces with the strategies, insights, and **cheat codes** I wish someone had given me.

It won't fix a system designed to work against us. But it will ensure that you're no longer moving mindlessly. It will arm you with the knowledge, positioning, and power moves to shift the game in your favor. **They NEVER meant for us to win.**

BlackPrint

Cheat Codes for Succeeding in Corporate America as a Black Professional

BlackPrint

Cheat Codes for Succeeding in Corporate America as a Black Professional

Introduction: Why This Book Exists

Let's get something straight from the jump: **Corporate America was NOT built for us.**

You already know that. You've felt it in meetings when your ideas were overlooked but repeated—and praised— by someone else five minutes later. You've seen it in the **leadership teams that rarely look like you**. You've watched as coworkers glide through the workplace with a level of ease that you know you can't afford.

This book is your **BlackPrint—your unfiltered guide** to navigating corporate America as a Black professional. It's about knowing the game, recognizing the rules they'll never say out loud, and developing the strategies to win anyway. Because here's the truth:

- **Your talent alone is not enough.**

- **Your work ethic alone is not enough.**

- **Even being the "best" won't always be enough.**

That's because the game is rigged. But if you understand the rules—and play your moves strategically—you can win on your own terms.

I've seen it firsthand. I've coached leaders, sat in executive meetings, and watched careers rise and fall—sometimes for reasons unrelated to performance. I've also navigated these spaces myself, learning (sometimes the hard way) what it really takes to survive and thrive.

This book is the cheat code I wish I had had when I started. It's the truth that mentors whisper behind closed doors. It's the advice that your white colleagues don't have to think about—but you absolutely do.

So, if you're tired of feeling like you're playing chess against people playing checkers, you're in the right place.

This book is not about surviving. **It's about winning.**

Let's get to it.

Chapter 1
No, You Cannot Do
What They Do

You may already know this, but you may not have fully admitted it: **You do not have the same margin for error as your white counterparts.**

You can't show up the same way they do. You **can't** get too comfortable. You **can't** make the same mistakes. And if you do, the consequences will not be the same.

Some people will say that's unfair. And they're right. **But fairness isn't the game being played.**

Welcome to the Double Standard

If you've been in corporate America for more than five minutes, you've seen it.

* A white colleague raises their voice in a meeting? They're seen as **passionate and assertive**.

* You do the same? You're aggressive and intimidating.

* A white coworker **shows up late?** It's brushed off as "Oh, traffic was wild today."

- You show up late? It's, *"Is everything okay at home?"* (Read: Can you handle this role?)

These are not exaggerations. **The bar is different for you...for us.** And no amount of talent, confidence, or qualifications will entirely change that reality.

Why You Can't "Just Be Yourself"

One of the biggest lies told to Black professionals is: **"Just be yourself, and you'll be fine."**

That advice works—for *them*. Not for you.

The truth is, **you have to be strategic about how you present yourself** at all times. Every move you make is being watched, measured, and **sometimes weaponized against you.** That doesn't mean you need to shrink yourself—it means you need to **play smart.**

Does that mean you can never let your guard down? Not exactly. But it does mean:

- Understand how you are perceived before you decide how to show up.

- Be intentional about your communication style.

8

- Don't assume that what works for others will work for you.

White employees have the privilege of **being individuals in the workplace**. If they mess up, it's just *their* mistake. **For us, one bad experience can shape how we—and other Black professionals after us—are viewed.**

That's why it's **critical to move with awareness**, precision, and a clear understanding of the game you're playing.

Corporate Cheat Codes: Winning in the Face of Double Standards

At the end of every chapter, you'll find these Corporate Cheat Codes—**direct, actionable strategies** to help you maneuver smarter in corporate spaces.

Cheat Code #1: Always Be Three Steps Ahead

If they have one plan, you need three.

- **Know the expectations**: Understand your job description and the *hidden* expectations that they'll never say out loud.

- **Anticipate the biases:** Be proactive in presenting your work, knowing that you may not get the same benefit of the doubt.

- **Have receipts:** Keep a record of your work, wins, and impact because when it's time for reviews or promotions, **you will need to advocate for yourself more than others do.**

Cheat Code #2: Watch How Others Fail (And Don't Do That)

- Pay attention to **who gets second chances—and who doesn't.**

- Take mental notes on what **behaviors get rewarded and which ones get penalized.**

- Learn from the mistakes of others so you don't have to make them yourself.

Cheat Code #3: Your Reputation is Currency, Protect It

- The higher you go, **the less your work speaks for itself**—and the more your reputation does.

- Avoid office drama, **be mindful of who you tru**st, and always control your **narrative**.

- Your brand is being built **with or without you,** so **make sure you're the one shaping it**.

What's Next?

Now that we've established the unspoken rules about the double standards you'll face, it's time to talk about the playing field itself. In the next chapter, we break down:

Understanding the Landscape—what corporate culture really looks like, how power operates, and why knowing who controls the room is just as important as knowing what's being said in it.

BlackPrint

Cheat Codes for Succeeding in Corporate America as a Black Professional

Chapter 2
Understand the Landscape

Welcome to the Gameboard

Imagine walking into a massive, high-stakes chess tournament—except no one tells you the rules. No one explains how the pieces move, what strategies work, or who your real opponents are. Worse, some players have been given a **head start**, while you're expected to **figure it out on your own**—with the *added* pressure of knowing that if you make the wrong move, it won't just be *your* game that suffers.

That's corporate America.

It's a complex, interconnected system where **power is distributed unevenly, rules aren't always written down, and the people in control are not always the smartest or most deserving—but they do know how the game is played.**

Your job?
Learn the board. Learn the players. **And then make the game work for you.**

13

Because here's the truth:

- **Corporate power isn't about titles—it's about control.** Some of the most influential people don't have the biggest offices.

- **Your reputation moves faster than you do.** People decide your value in rooms you haven't even entered yet.

- **Knowing the rules isn't enough**—you need to understand how they shift for people who look like you.

If you don't understand how the system works, you'll keep getting blindsided by decisions that affect you.

Let's break it down.

The Four Corporate Power Zones

Corporate power isn't one-size-fits-all. It comes in different forms, and if you don't recognize who has it— and how they use it—**you're playing the game blind.**

1. The Decision-Makers (Real Power)

- **Who They Are:** Executives, VPs, Board Members

- **What They Control:** Strategy, budgets, promotions, layoffs.

- **Why They Matter:** They don't just approve raises—they control the entire table you're trying to sit at. **If you want to move up, you need at least one of these people in your corner.**

Real Talk: If you want to move up, at least one of these people needs to know your name and respect your work.

2. The Gatekeepers (Positional Power)

- **Who They Are:** These are the middle managers, HR leaders, and senior directors who control access to opportunities. They don't necessarily make the big decisions, but they **influence who gets considered** for them.

- **What They Control:** Hiring, project assignments, policy enforcement

- **Why They Matter:** If a **gatekeeper doesn't like you,** they can quietly stall your career—without you even realizing it. They won't promote you themselves, but they will decide whether your name even makes it to the conversation.

Real Talk: If a gatekeeper doesn't like you, your career is in quicksand—**you won't even know the opportunities you're missing.**

3. The Influencers (Social Power)

- **Who They Are:** Culture leaders, long-tenured employees, "connectors" and leaders people listen to They are not always in leadership, but their relationships give them power.

- **What They Control:** Office dynamics, team perceptions, informal decision-making.

- **Why They Matter:** They shape the narrative about who's "ready" for leadership. If they **vouch for you,** doors will open. If they don't, **your name may never even come up.**

Real Talk: If an influencer likes you, they **will advocate for you in rooms you'll never see.** Many Black professionals ignore this group, but trust me—**they see everything. And they remember.**

4. The Silent Observers (Hidden Power)

- **Who They Are:** These are **the people who watch from the sidelines**—the quiet analysts, the HR reps taking notes, the admin assistants who hear everything.

- **What They Control:** They may not have direct power, **but they influence the narrative** in subtle, unexpected ways. Who gets invited where, what feedback gets documented, and who **"seems like a good fit."**

- Why They Matter: You'd be shocked how many "little conversations" shape significant career decisions.

Real Talk: Some of the most **career-altering decisions** come from **private conversations** between **people you aren't even thinking about.**

The Gameboard: How Power Moves

Now that you know the players, let's talk about how **the system actually works.**

Corporate power **isn't just about who's the boss**—it's about how **influence, control, and decision-making actually happen behind closed doors.**

Here's what you need to know:

1. Not All Leaders Have Power (And Not All Powerful People Are Leaders)

- Some **VPs and Directors** have **titles but no real control**—they just follow orders from above.

- Some **individual contributors** (especially those who've been in the company forever) **can get things done faster than your boss ever could.**

- The key is figuring out who actually moves things forward.

Cheat Code: Watch who people go to for approval, even when they don't have to. That's real power.

2. Your Reputation Moves Faster Than You Do

- Before you get promoted, people will **already have opinions about you.**

- The higher up you go, the less decisions are made on numbers and the more they're based on perception.

- If people **trust you, respect you, and see you as valuable,** opportunities will come your way before you even ask.

Cheat Code: Curate your corporate brand—your name should be attached to excellence, reliability, and strategic thinking.

3. Culture is Power (And It's Not Always in the Employee Handbook)

- Every company has an **official culture** (what they put on the website) and a **real culture** (what actually happens).

- Failing to read the real culture means you'll **misstep without even knowing why.**

- If a company values politics, then playing fair won't help you. If a company values quiet loyalty, then being too loud too soon could backfire.

Cheat Code: Study who gets rewarded and who gets sidelined. That will tell you the real culture.

That's where we're going next.

Corporate Cheat Code: Controlling Your Position on the Board

Now that you understand the landscape, here's how to move strategically:

Cheat Code #1: Map Your Corporate Network

- Identify **who holds power** in your company (Decision-Makers, Gatekeepers, Influencers, and Observers).

- Build relationships with people in all four zones—not just those above you.

- If you don't know who the power players are, you are already behind.

Cheat Code #2: Play the Long Game

- Don't just focus on today's job—position yourself for your next opportunity.

- Align yourself with **high-impact projects** that get noticed by Decision-Makers.

- Don't burn bridges, **even if you leave a company**—influential people move around, and they *talk*.

Cheat Code #3: Manage Perception as Much as Performance

- Your **work alone will not get you promoted**—how people **perceive you** is equally (if not more) important.

- If people see you as **"just a hard worker"** but not as a strategic thinker, you will get stuck.

- Make sure your contributions **align with leadership priorities**—not just your to-do list.

BlackPrint

Cheat Codes for Succeeding in Corporate America as a Black Professional

Chapter 3
How You See Yourself
vs. How You're Seen

The Reality of Perception

Let's start here:

There's who you think you are and who they've decided you are. Two separate identities. They are two very different worlds. And the gap between those two versions of you can make or break your corporate journey.

You may see yourself as ambitious, strategic, a strong communicator, and a natural leader. However, how you see yourself is only half the battle because perception in corporate America is reality.

If the right people don't see those same qualities in you, you're not going anywhere fast. And sometimes, even when they do, it's filtered through biases, stereotypes, and preconceived notions.

So, let's break down exactly what that means—and what you can do about it.

The Invisible Mirror

What You See vs. What They See

Here's a real-life scenario you might recognize:

You're passionate about your work.

You speak up in meetings because you care deeply about outcomes. But to others, you might be perceived as **"aggressive," "overly emotional," or worse— "difficult."**

This is especially true for **Black professionals and even more pronounced for Black women.** The things that might get your colleagues celebrated often become reasons you're sidelined or overlooked.

- When your white colleague takes initiative, they're **proactive**.

- When you do the same, you're **seen as pushy**.

- They make mistakes, and it's **just part of the job**.

- You make a mistake, and it's a **"development opportunity"** that holds you back from promotions.

Sound familiar? The question isn't just whether these perceptions are fair (**spoiler alert: they're not**). The question is, what do you **do about it?**

Why Perception Matters More Than You Think

In corporate spaces, how you are seen determines:

- Whether you're selected for projects

- Your promotions and raises

- Your access to mentors and sponsors

- Ultimately, your career trajectory

You have **far less control over how people see you than you realize.** But you **can** influence and manage that perception—strategically.

Owning Your Narrative

If you don't define your narrative, **someone else will**—and I promise you, it will not be in your favor. Here are three powerful ways to take control of your narrative immediately:

1. The Power of Strategic Visibility

Visibility matters more than performance. If no one sees your wins, **do they really count?**

- **Highlight your wins proactively:** Don't assume your manager notices or appreciates your work. Clearly communicate your achievements in ways that align with organizational goals.

- **Speak strategically:** Contribute in meetings, but know the difference between "speaking up" and "over-sharing." Always ask yourself: "Does this add value? Does this demonstrate my capability clearly?"

2. Reading Perceptions (Before They Hurt You)

You must know how others perceive you to navigate successfully. Here's how:

- **Seek Truthful Feedback (But Take It with a Grain of Salt)**
  - **Get feedback—but filter it carefully.** Not all feedback is created equal, especially when biases come into play.

o   Ask people whose judgment you trust and who have demonstrated fairness and objectivity.

Remember: Feedback is about **perception,** not necessarily fact. But if **multiple trusted sources share the same observation, pay attention.**

Leveraging Perception to Your Advantage

Perception isn't always your enemy—it can also be your most powerful tool.

Amplify Positive Perceptions

*   **Identify what you're already known for.** Are you reliable, strategic, or collaborative? Lean into these strengths and amplify them publicly.

*   **Create advocates who reinforce your narrative.** When others publicly affirm your strengths, perceptions shift faster.

The Cheat Code: Ask influential colleagues to highlight your contributions or strengths publicly in meetings or communications. Their endorsement is powerful currency.

Corporate Cheat Codes: Bridging the Perception Gap

You can't control everyone's perception, but you can influence it strategically:

Cheat Code #1: The Mirror Check

- **Regularly assess your reputation.** What are the top three words others would use to describe you at work?

- **If they aren't the three words you want, redefine your strategy immediately.** Ask yourself: "What behaviors do I need to shift to move perception closer to reality?"

Cheat Code #2: Your Allies Are Your Mirrors

- Identify **trusted allies** who can give you unfiltered insights about your reputation.

- **Listen** carefully and **without defensiveness**—these insights are your competitive advantage.

Cheat Code #3: Strategic Visibility

- **Visibility is power—use it wisely.** Choose carefully when, where, and how you show up.

- If you aren't regularly in front of influential people, you're invisible. Be strategic about the moments you choose to shine and the messages you send.

Final Thoughts

This game is played on perception, and you've got to play smart. Yes, it's exhausting. Yes, it can feel unfair. But this isn't about fairness—it's about making strategic moves so that perception **works for you, not against you.**

The good news? **Once you master the game of perception, you're playing at an entirely new level.**

BlackPrint

Cheat Codes for Succeeding in Corporate America as a Black Professional

Chapter 4
Not All Seats at the Table Are Created Equal

The Illusion of Inclusion

You made it.

You finally got that **promotion, seat in leadership, or invitation to the big meeting**. You look around the table, feeling like all your hard work has paid off.

Then, reality sets in.

- You're in the room, but your voice isn't being heard.

- Your input is acknowledged but never acted on.

- You're there but feel like a **symbol, not a decision-maker.**

That's when you realize that **not every seat at the table holds the same weight**. Some are meant to drive **decisions,** while others exist to check a diversity box.

This chapter is about recognizing the difference between real power and performative inclusion—and how to ensure your seat *actually* counts.

The Three Types of Seats in Corporate Spaces

1. The Seat with Influence (Power Seat)

Who Sits Here?

- Key decision-makers

- Leaders who drive strategy, policy, and promotions

- People whose words and ideas move the company forward

What It Means

- You don't just sit at the table; y**our voice carries weight.**

- You have **direct access** to decision-making processes.

Cheat Code: If you're **not in these seats yet,** your goal is to **align with the people who are.** Build relationships, get invited to key conversations, and show your strategic thinking when it matters most.

2. The Seat as a Token (Symbolic Seat)

Who Sits Here?

- The **only** Black person in leadership
- "Diversity hires" who were **brought in to be seen, not heard**
- Employees placed in leadership without **real decision-making power**

What It Means

- You're in the room b**ut not included in real conversations**
- Your presence is meant to **give the appearance of diversity**, not drive change

Cheat Code: If you realize you're in a **Symbolic Seat**, don't just accept it. **Start strategically shifting into real influence.** Speak on key issues, align with power players, and make moves that **force them to take you seriously.**

3. The Seat That's a Trap (Set-Up Seat)

Who Sits Here?

- Black professionals who are placed in **high-risk, high-visibility roles with limited support**

- Leaders brought in to **clean up a mess**—but blamed if it fails

- People given **responsibility without authority**

What It Means

- You're given a **role that looks like power but is a setup for failure.**

- You're expected to **fix broken systems without the resources needed to succeed.**

- If things go wrong, **you take the fall**—but if they go right, the credit goes elsewhere.

Cheat Code: If you're placed in a Set-Up Seat, ask yourself:

1. Do I have the resources, support, and authority to succeed in this role?

2. Who benefits if I fail?

3. What safeguards can I put in place to protect my name and reputation?

This **"opportunity" might be a landmine. Proceed with caution.**

How to Turn Your Seat Into Power

So, you've gotten a seat—but how do you make sure it matters? Here's how:

1. Speak With Strategy, Not Just Volume

- Being heard is **not about talking the most**—it's about speaking **at the right time, with the right message, to the right people.**

- **Frame your points in ways leadership values.** Example: Instead of "We need more DEI efforts," try **"Here's how DEI directly impacts retention and profitability."**

Cheat Code: Tie your ideas to business priorities. That's how you make leadership listen.

2. Build Relationships with Decision-Makers

- Influence isn't just about **what you say in meetings** —it's also about **who is willing to advocate for you behind closed doors.**

- If key leaders don't **know, trust, or respect you**, your impact will always be limited.

Cheat Code: Identify **who holds real power and start aligning yourself with them** through mentorship, collaboration, and visibility.

3. Document Your Contributions

- If you don't keep a **paper trail** of your wins, don't expect anyone else to.

- **When introducing an idea, follow up with an email:** "As discussed in the meeting, I suggested X to improve Y. *Looking forward to the next steps.*"

- This creates **receipts** in case someone tries to claim or erase your impact.

Cheat Code: Your **work should have your fingerprints on it**—so that your contributions are undeniable even when you're not in the room.

Corporate Cheat Codes: Owning Your Seat at the Table

Cheat Code #1: Assess Your Seat—Then Move Accordingly

- Are you in a **Power Seat, Symbolic Seat, or Set-Up Seat?** Be honest about where you stand.

- Start strategizing your path to real influence, whether it's symbolic or a trap.

Cheat Code #2: Make Yourself Undeniable

- Speak in a way that **forces decision-makers to listen.**

- Align your work with the company's **most important goals** so that ignoring you becomes a business risk.

Cheat Code #3: Leverage the Room, Even If You're Not Fully Included

- **Observe the dynamics.** Who talks the most? Who actually gets listened to? Who gets credit?

- **Play the long game.** If you're not in a decision-making role, **position yourself so that the next move is yours.**

Final Thoughts

This game isn't just about getting in the room. It's about **owning your space, making power moves, and refusing to be a silent figure at someone else's table.**

If they gave you a seat without power, you've got two choices:

1. **Make that seat powerful** by changing the game.

2. **Build your own damn table.**

Either way, you're not here just to decorate the room. You're here to **shift the room.**

What's Next?

Now that we've covered **how to make your seat matter,** we're heading into one of the **most important chapters yet:**

Chapter 5: What You Don't Know WILL Hurt You

- The **career-limiting mistakes** Black professionals make (**without realizing it**)

- The **unspoken corporate rules** that can stall or accelerate your growth

- How to **move smartly so you don't sabotage your own career**

This next one is about **what they won't tell you—but what you *must* know.**

BlackPrint

Cheat Codes for Succeeding in Corporate America as a Black Professional

Chapter 5

What You Don't Know
WILL Hurt You

The Career Killers No One Warns You About

You've heard the saying:

"What you don't know won't hurt you."

Well, in corporate America? **That's a lie.**

What you **don't know will**:

- **Stall your career** while others move ahead.

- **Make you think you're doing well,** until you're blindsided at review time.

- **Cost you promotions, raises, and opportunities;** without you even realizing why.

The truth is that **Black professionals aren't just judged on performance—we're judged on how well we navigate the *unspoken* rules of the game.**

And most of these rules?

Nobody is going to sit you down and tell you.

So, I'm going to tell you.

Five Silent Career Killers You Need to Know

1. **Believing Hard Work** Alone Will Get **You Promoted**

- **Let's be clear: Hard work** is the **minimum expectation.**

  o Does it get you noticed? **Nope.**

  o Guarantees advancement? **Not even close.**

  o Keeps you employed? Maybe... **until they decide otherwise**.

Here's the real game:

Promotions aren't just about performance, they are about **visibility, relationships,** and alignment with **leadership priorities.**

If leadership does not see you as **strategic, influential, or "leadership material,"** you're getting skipped over.

Cheat Code: Make sure the right people know your impact. You can work in **silence** if you want, but **don't expect silence to lead to success**.

2. Thinking Your Work Speaks for Itself

Your work does not **"speak for itself."**

People speak for it.

And if the right people aren't talking about your work, you are invisible.

White professionals **have built-in networks and sponsors** who advocate for them. Black professionals? We often assume if we just **"do the work,"** we'll get recognized.

Cheat Code: You need advocates, not just effort.

- Build relationships with **decision-makers**.

- Make sure your **wins are seen, documented, and strategically shared.**

3. Ignoring Office Politics (Because You "Don't Do Politics")

I get it. Nobody likes corporate politics. But here's the hard truth:

- You **don't** have to **like** the game.

- You **don't** even have to **respect** the game.

- But you **DO need to know how it's played**—or you'll lose by default.

Corporate politics **aren't about drama—they're about influence.** If you ignore them, **you're voluntarily giving up power.**

Cheat Code: Identify who actually controls decisions. It's not always the person with the biggest title. **Align yourself with the real power players.**

4. **Not Controlling Your Narrative:**

If you don't **actively shape** how people **see** you, they will define you however *they want*.

Cheat Code: Know your corporate reputation—before it becomes a problem.

And guess what? Their version might not be flattering.

- If you're not careful, you get labeled as **"too quiet"** or **"not leadership material."**

- If you are too assertive, you get labeled as **"intimidating"** or **"not a team player."**

- If you only work hard and keep your head down, you get *forgotten*.

- Ask trusted colleagues how you're perceived.

- If the perception doesn't match who you are or want to be, it's time to shift it strategically.

4. **Failing to Build a Personal Board of Directors**

You need a Personal Board of Directors:

White professionals **have built-in networks**—mentors, sponsors, advocates who open doors for them.

Black professionals? **We often try to go at it alone.** And that's a mistake.

- **A Mentor** – Gives advice and guidance

- **A Sponsor** – Puts your name in the right rooms

- **A Peer Ally** – Keeps you informed and connected

- **A Trusted Advisor** – Helps you navigate tricky situations

Cheat Code: If you don't have these people in your corner, start building your network *NOW*. The higher you go, the **less you can succeed alone.**

Corporate Cheat Codes: Moving Smarter, Not Harder

Cheat Code #1: Keep a "Brag Sheet"

- Keep a **running document of your wins, significant contributions, and positive feedback.**

- When performance review season comes, **you'll have receipts.**

Cheat Code #2: Know the Promotion Cycle

- Most promotions **are decided months before they're announced.**

- If you're waiting until review season to prove yourself, **you're too late.**

- Find out **when decisions are made and start positioning yourself** before that.

Cheat Code #3: Play the Long Game

- Every move should be **intentional.**

- Before you take on more work, ask:

  o Does this **align with my career goals?**

  o Will this put me **in front of decision-makers?**

o   Is this a stepping stone or just extra work with no discernible benefit?

Smart moves, **not just hard work,** win the game.

Final Thoughts

This chapter is the truth that corporate America **won't** tell you.

We've all seen talented Black professionals **stuck in the same roles for years** while less qualified people move ahead. **It's not because they aren't working hard.** It's because they **didn't know the hidden rules.**

Now, you do. And **once you see the game, you cannot unsee it.**

This is how you **stop playing checkers while they are playing chess.**

What's Next?

Now that we've exposed the unspoken rules, it's time to talk about something even more significant:

Chapter 6: "It's About So Much More Than Performance"

- Why **your work alone won't get you where you want to go**

- The **unwritten expectations of leadership**

- How to **position yourself as "next in line" for major roles**

This next chapter is all about **making the shift from worker to leader**—because your career isn't just about what you do, it's about what you represent.

Chapter 6

It's About So Much *More* Than Performance

The Hard Truth: Doing the Work Won't Be Enough

If you've been in corporate America for any amount of time, you've probably noticed something:

- The **most hardworking people** aren't always the ones getting promoted.

- **The most talented employees** aren't necessarily the highest paid.

- And the **most qualified candidates** often get passed over for leadership roles.

That's because **success at work isn't just about how well you perform.** It's about **who sees your performance, who values it, and who is willing to advocate for your next step.**

The sooner you shift your mindset from **"If I just work hard, they'll see my value"** to **"I need to be strategic**

49

about how I position myself," the sooner you'll start moving up. This is where we break free from **Proving Mode** and step into **Positioning Mode.**

Proving Mode vs. Positioning Mode: The Shift That Changes Everything

Proving Mode (Where Most Black Professionals Get Stuck)

- Constantly **grinding to "prove"** you deserve to be here
- Taking on **extra work, long hours, and endless projects**
- Believing that if **you work hard enough, someone will notice and reward you**
- Feeling frustrated when **less talented people get ahead**

Positioning Mode (Where Leaders Operate)

- Being **strategic about visibility, relationships**, and influence
- Taking on **high-value work** that aligns with leadership priorities (not just "extra" work)
- Ensuring the **right people know your impact**

50

- Playing the **long game—not just trying to be the best worker but positioning yourself for leadership**

Bottom Line: If you spend all your energy proving yourself, you're **not positioning yourself to move up.**

The Three Things That Matter More Than Performance

If performance alone determined success, **workplaces would look very different.** But that's not how this game works.

Here's what actually drives career growth:

1. Perception: How They See You Determines How Far You Go

Hard truth: Being "good at your job" is not the same as being seen as "leadership material." **If leadership doesn't perceive you as someone who can operate at a higher level, you will not be invited into higher spaces**—no matter how excellent your work is.

Cheat Code: Start acting, speaking, and showing up as the role you want, before you even have it. The moment leadership sees you differently, opportunities follow.

2. Alignment: Your Work Needs to Match Leadership Priorities

Most people assume their job is to do what's assigned to them. **Wrong.** Your job is determining what leadership values most and aligning your work accordingly.

Cheat Codes:

- Pay attention to **what gets celebrated and funded.**

- Look at **who's getting promoted and why.**

- Ensure **your work directly impacts leadership goals**—otherwise, you're grinding for nothing.

3. Sponsorship: Who Advocates for You Behind Closed Doors?

At a certain point in your career, promotions don't happen because you **applied for a job**—they happen because **someone put your name in the right room.** You're already behind if you don't have **at least one influential sponsor** advocating for you when you're not around.

Cheat Code: Build relationships with **decision-makers** and **high-level mentors**. If your name isn't being mentioned in the right places, **you're invisible**.

How to Move from Worker to Leader

If you're ready to step into **Positioning Mode**, here's how you start:

Speak Strategically, Not Just Frequently

- Every time you open your mouth in a meeting, ask yourself:

  - Am I just **talking**—or am I **adding value**?

  - Is this moving me closer to leadership perception?

Stop Accepting Every Extra Task

- Being **the go-to person for extra work** does not make you a leader.

- Being **the go-to person for strategic initiatives** does.

- Before you take on more, ask: *Does this align with where I'm trying to go?*

Make Your Impact Visible

- If your boss had to **pitch your promotion tomorrow**, would they have **clear, undeniable proof of your value?**

- If not, start documenting **your wins, impact, and how your work drives business success.**

Corporate Cheat Codes: Mastering Positioning Mode

Cheat Code #1: Own Your Executive Presence

- Leadership isn't just about what you do but how you carry yourself.

- Walk, talk, and operate like a leader before you have the title.

Cheat Code #2: Align Your Work with Power Moves

- **Every task isn't equal.** Prioritize work that puts you in front of decision-makers.

- Attach your work to **profitability, efficiency, and business growth**. That's what leaders care about.

Cheat Code #3: Build Influence, Not Just Skills

- Skills will get you in the door. **Influence** will get you in the rooms where decisions are made.

- **Who knows, trusts, and respects you?** That's more important than any certification or extra workload.

Final Thoughts

This is the information most Black professionals never get told about. We spend **too much time proving our** worth when we should be **positioning ourselves** for leadership.

Hard truth: If you're still focused on being the best worker in the room, you're playing small. It's time to move differently.

You're not just here to work. **You're here to lead.**

What's Next?

Now that we've made the **Proving Mode** → **Positioning Mode shift,** we're going straight into:

Chapter 7: Sponsors Matter

- The difference between mentors and sponsors

- Why having a sponsor is the #1 career accelerator

- How to find and secure a powerful sponsor to open doors for you

This next chapter is **crucial**—because talent gets you noticed, but sponsorship gets you **promoted**.

Chapter 7
Sponsors Matter

Why Mentors Help You Grow, but Sponsors Get You Promoted

Let's clear this up:

* A mentor advises you. A **sponsor ADVOCATES** for you.

* A mentor guides your career. A **sponsor ELEVATES** your career.

* A mentor helps you plan. A **sponsor** makes sure your name is in the **right rooms**.

Here's the hard truth: **If you don't have a sponsor, your career moves will always be slower and more complicated than they need to be.**

Why?

Because at a **certain level, promotions aren't about applications**—they're about **conversations happening behind closed doors.**

57

The people getting those big opportunities? They didn't just work hard.

Someone **with power** made sure they were considered. That's what a sponsor does.

And if you don't have one? **You're already behind.**

Mentors vs. Sponsors: The Career Game-Changer

Most people are told to **find a mentor**. That's cute. But if you want to **move up and move fast**? You need a **sponsor**.

What Mentors Do

- Give **advice**

- Share **wisdom and guidance**

- Help you **think through career decisions**

- Provide **perspective, not power**

Mentors are valuable but won't necessarily get you to the next level.

What Sponsors Do

- Put your name in the **right rooms**

- **Advocate for you** in leadership discussions

- **Open doors** that would otherwise be closed

- Use their influence to **create opportunities for you**

A sponsor doesn't just help you prepare for leadership—they make sure leadership sees you as ready.

Bottom Line: A mentor helps you **navigate the game.** A sponsor **changes the game for you.**

Why Sponsorship is a Career Accelerator

- **FACT:** At a certain point, your next promotion **is not about your skills** but about leadership's confidence in you.

- **FACT:** Sponsorship is often the **#1 deciding factor** in who moves up.

- **FACT:** Most Black professionals are **OVER-MENTORED** but **UNDER-SPONSORED.**

Let's sit on that last one for a second.

Many of us have mentors **who give us guidance,** but we don't have sponsors **fighting for our names to be on the shortlist when big opportunities arise.**

That gap is why so many **high-performing Black professionals stay stuck at mid-level positions** instead of moving into leadership.

Cheat Code: If you've been working hard but getting overlooked, the question is:

"WHO in leadership is actively advocating for me?" If you can't name someone, it's **time to fix that.**

How to Attract and Secure a Powerful Sponsor

- Sponsorship isn't about asking for favors.
- It's about creating relationships where influential people see you as worth investing in.

Here's how you make that happen:

1. Identify Who Has Real Influence

Not every executive is a power player. Some have big titles but no real sway, while others don't have the most prominent titles but control major decisions.

Cheat Code: Watch for whom people go to for **approvals, advice, and final decisions**—those are the sponsors you want.

2. Make Yourself Sponsorable

You can't just **walk up to someone and ask them to be your sponsor**. Sponsorship is **earned**.

How do you attract a sponsor?

- **Be visible**—your work must be known, **not just done.**

- **Be valuable**—solve problems that matter to leadership.

- **Be consistent**—a sponsor must feel **confident putting their name on the line for you.**

Cheat Code: Ask yourself: *Would I vouch for me in a high-stakes meeting?* If not, you have work to do.

3. Get in Their Orbit

Sponsors don't sponsor people they don't know.

If you want to build sponsorship, you have to:

- **Be in the rooms they're in** (high-visibility projects, leadership meetings, committees)

- **Find ways to work with them** (volunteer for initiatives they care about)

61

- **Engage with their work** (comment on their insights, ask strategic questions)

Cheat Code: Be intentional about creating proximity. The more they see you operating at a high level, the more they'll naturally start advocating for you.

4. Have the "Sponsorship Conversation" (Strategically)

Once a leader **knows your value**, you can directly discuss sponsorship.

Example:

"I admire how you've navigated leadership. I'd love to learn from you and get your perspective on how to grow into my next role. Would you be open to a conversation about that?"

That's **non-threatening and strategic, opening the door** without putting pressure on them.

Cheat Code: The **best sponsors choose you** before you ask. The **conversation happens naturally** *if* you've built a strong relationship and shown value.

BlackPrint

Cheat Codes for Succeeding in Corporate America as a Black Professional

Corporate Cheat Codes: Making Sponsorship Work for You

Cheat Code #1: Understand That Sponsorship Is a Two-Way Street

- A sponsor is **putting their reputation on the line for you. Make** sure you **make them look good.**

- The stronger your performance, the more willing they will be to advocate for you.

Cheat Code #2: Build Multiple Sponsorship Relationships

- Don't rely on **just one person.**

- You need **a network of sponsors** who can advocate for you in different spaces.

Cheat Code #3: Be Ready When the Opportunity Comes

- Sponsorship **creates opportunities**, but you have to **be prepared when they appear.**

- Make sure you're **operating at the next level** BEFORE you get promoted.

Final Thoughts

Having a sponsor is the difference between hoping for a promotion and being positioned for one.

If you want to accelerate your career, ask yourself: *"Who in power is actively invested in my success?"*

If the answer is no one—it's time to change that **immediately.**

What's Next?

Now that we've established the **power of sponsorship**, it's time to go even deeper into strategy.

Chapter 8: Metered & Measured Matters

* Why **Black professionals have to be more strategic about how they show up**

* How to **control your energy, tone, and delivery** in corporate spaces

* Mastering "executive presence" **without feeling like you have to shrink yourself**

This one is all about **playing the long game—making intentional, measured moves that keep you in control of your career.**

BlackPrint

Cheat Codes for Succeeding in Corporate America as a Black Professional

Chapter 8
Metered & Measured Matters

Every Move You Make Sends a Message

In corporate spaces, you are **constantly being watched.** Your tone, body language, facial expressions, and how you speak up—or don't.

It all sends a message. For Black professionals, that message is often **interpreted before we even open our mouths.** This chapter is about mastering **precision, perception, and executive presence** so that every move you make is **intentional, strategic, and undeniable.**

Why Every Move Must Be Intentional

The Unfair Truth: You Will Be Read Differently

We've seen it happen:

* A **white colleague** can be **blunt**—they're seen as **"assertive."**

* A **Black woman** does the same—she's labeled **"aggressive."**

- A **white man** can be passionate in a meeting—they call it **"leadership."**
- A **Black man** does the same—they call it "intimidating."

This is <u>not</u> paranoia—it's **pattern recognition.**

The reality is that **you and I don't get the same margin for error.** So, your words, tone, and presence must be **measured, metered, and powerful.**

Mastering "Executive Presence" Without Shrinking Yourself

Some people will tell you to "just be yourself" at work.

That's not true. You must be strategic if you want to lead.

Executive presence isn't about changing who you are —it's about **controlling** how you are **perceived.**

It's about **learning how to command rooms, influence decisions, and ensure that when you speak, people listen.**

Here's how to make that happen:

1. **Control Your Tone—Because It's Being Read, Whether You Like It or Not**

The way you say something matters just as much as what you say.

The wrong tone—too harsh, defensive, and blunt—can overshadow your message entirely.

Cheat Code: Deliver every message with control, clarity, and confidence.

* Want to push back? Say: *"**I see it differently. Here's why.**"* (Not "That doesn't make sense .")

* Need to redirect the conversation? Say: *"**Let's refocus on the bigger goal**"* (Not "We're getting off track .")

Same message, different impact.

2. **Be Deliberate With Your Body Language**

Your body speaks before you do.

Ever notice how people in power **take up space**? They walk in like they belong there. They sit at the table **with certainty.**

Cheat Code: Walk into every room like you have a right to be there—because you do.

- Sit with **confidence**—don't shrink into yourself.

- **Make eye contact** when you speak—it conveys certainty.

- **Control your reactions**. A raised eyebrow, a sigh, or a sudden shift in posture can change the energy in the room.

3. Learn the Art of the Strategic Pause

Silence is power.

The loudest person in the room isn't always the most influential. The one who **speaks with precision and purpose?** That's the leader.

Cheat Code: Use **strategic pauses** before responding. It makes people lean in.

- **Example:**

  o **Instant reaction:** "I don't think that's the right approach."

  o **Strategic pause:** (silent beat, then...) "There's another angle we might want to consider."

That pause forces the room to focus on you. **It signals confidence.**

4. **Don't Just Speak—Command Attention.** Your voice is a tool, use it wisely.

Cheat Code: Master the three levels of power speech:

o **Calm & Controlled:** For everyday discussions. (Steady, measured tone.)

o **Authoritative & Clear:** For key moments. (Firm, confident delivery.)

o **Deliberate & Impactful**: For leadership presence. (Slow, intentional, powerful.)

Leaders **don't rush their words**—they speak in a way that **demands attention.**

Corporate Cheat Codes: Mastering Metered & Measured Moves

Cheat Code #1: Read the Room Before You Move

* Every room has a **power dynamic**. Before you speak, **observe.**

* Who is leading? Who has influence? Who gets cut off, and who gets listened to?

Cheat Code #2: When in Doubt, Say Less—But Make It Count

- Too much talking can dilute your power.

- Be **concise, clear, and intentional**—make every word carry weight.

Cheat Code #3: Match Your Communication to the Culture

- Some workplaces value **directness**. Others prefer a diplomatic approach.

- Pay attention to **how leadership communicates and adapt accordingly.**

Final Thoughts

This chapter is next-level strategy.

You are always being perceived, so **make sure you control the perception**.

Every move you make **should reinforce your authority, confidence, and leadership presence**. This is how you ensure that when you speak, you're not just heard—you're respected.

What's Next?

Now that we've locked in executive presence, we're diving into:

Chapter 9: What Performance Reviews Are Really About

- Why performance reviews are **NOT just about performance**
- The **hidden factors** that determine your rating
- How to make sure your review positions you for **your next big move**

This next chapter is about playing the corporate review system to your advantage.

BlackPrint

Cheat Codes for Succeeding in Corporate America as a Black Professional

Chapter 9
What Performance Reviews Are *Really* About

Let's Be Clear. Your Performance Review is **NOT Just About Performance.**

You've been **working** hard all year.

You've **hit your goals**. Maybe even **exceeded them.** You walk into your performance review expecting to be recognized, rewarded, and **maybe even positioned for a promotion.**

But then—**BOOM.**

- Your rating is **lower than expected.**

- Your manager **hits you with "areas for growth"** that **were never mentioned before.**

- You're told **you're "doing great work,"** but there's no raise or promotion on the table.

What happened?

You just found out the **hard way** that performance reviews are **not just about what you do**.

Performance reviews are about the three Ps:

- **Perception** (how leadership sees you)

- **Politics** (who is advocating for you when you're not in the room)

- **Positioning** (whether they see you as ready for the next level)

If you're **not actively managing** this process, you leave **your career in someone else's hands. Let's fix that.**

The Hidden Truths About Performance Reviews

Truth #1: Your Rating is Often Decided Before the Review Even Happens

When you sit down for your review, your rating is already locked in.

- It's **not** based on what you just did.

- It's **not** about your last big project.

- It's based on a narrative built about you over time.

Cheat Code: You must **manage your review year-round**—not just when review season hits.

- Make sure **your manager sees your impact MONTHLY.**

- Keep a **Brag Sheet** of your wins so you can control the **story being told about you.**

- Have quarterly career check-ins so nothing in your review is a surprise.

Truth #2: Feedback is NOT Always About Facts; It's About Perception

Many Black professionals hear the same vague feedback in reviews:

- "You're doing **great work** but need to be **more visible."**

- "You should **work on your leadership presence.**"

- "You're **not quite ready for the next level.**"

What does any of that actually mean?

It means you're being judged on perception, not performance.

Cheat Code: Clarify feedback on the spot.

- **Ask:** "Can you give me a specific example?"

- **Ask:** "How are you measuring that?"

- **Ask:** "What would 'ready for the next level' look like in clear terms?"

- **Make them** define the goalposts—**so they can't keep moving them.**

Truth #3: The Performance Review is a Test, and Some People Already Have the Answers

Many white professionals get coached on how to prepare for their reviews.

They know what their manager values, the language to use, and how to position their work to align with company priorities.

Black professionals? **We're often expected to just "work hard" and hope for the best.**

Cheat Code: Treat your performance review like a strategic pitch.

- Know what **success looks like** in leadership's eyes.

- Frame your impact in terms of business value.

- Use language that aligns with company goals.

Do NOT assume your work will "speak for itself." You need to be the one speaking.

How to Control Your Performance Review

1. **Start Managing Your Review MONTHS in Advance.** If you wait until review season, you're too late.

Cheat Code: Have check-ins every quarter.

- **Ask:** "How am I tracking toward my goals?"

- **Ask:** "What would make me stand out as a top performer?"

- **Ask:** "What are leadership's biggest priorities right now?"

This keeps you in control and eliminates surprises.

2. **Keep a "Brag Sheet" of Your Wins**

o Your manager is not tracking all your accomplishments—**you need to do that.**

Cheat Code: Keep a personal document with:

- Major projects you led or contributed to

- Positive feedback from leadership or peers

- **Metrics** that show your impact (**revenue, efficiency, cost savings**)

o When review time comes, you have the receipts.

3. Use Strategic Language in Your Self-Evaluation

Your self-evaluation is not the time to be humble.

Cheat Code: Use power phrases that align your work with leadership goals:

- **Instead of:** "I worked on X project."

- **Say:** "I led a key initiative that improved efficiency by 20%, aligning with our department's strategic goal of operational excellence."

Speak their language so they see your impact in the way that matters to them.

4. Address Unfair or Biased Feedback with Strategy, Not Emotion

If you get unfair or biased feedback, do NOT just accept it.

Cheat Code: Push back professionally and strategically.

- o **Ask: "Can we clarify** how that feedback aligns with company success metrics?"

- o **Ask: "Can you provide examples** where I didn't demonstrate that skill?"

- o **Ask: "What specific actions** would you like to see from me in the next quarter?"

  a. This forces leadership to be accountable for their words.

  b. **Know the Promotion Timeline**—So You're Not Too Late

  c. Most promotions are **decided before they're announced.**

Cheat Code: Find out when decisions are made— and start positioning yourself early.

- o If promotions are discussed in **Q4, start planting seeds early in Q1.**

o Make sure **leaders know your name before decisions are made.**

You're already behind if you wait until review season to advocate for yourself.

Corporate Cheat Codes: Mastering the Review Process

Cheat Code #1: Manage Your Narrative All Year, Not Just at Review Time

- Keep track of your accomplishments in real time.

- Make sure your manager is aware of your contributions before review season.

Cheat Code #2: Align Your Work With What Leadership Cares About

- If leadership is **focused on revenue, frame your impact in financial terms.**

- If leadership is **focused on innovation, highlight how you've driven new ideas.**

Cheat Code #3: Secure Advocates Before the Review Cycle Starts

- Make sure key leaders know your name and impact before decisions are made.

- If your manager isn't pushing you, find a sponsor who will.

Final Thoughts

Performance reviews are **NOT** just about how well you work—they're about how well you position yourself.

If you **actively manage the process**, you can make sure every review puts you in a position for:

- **Raises**
- **Promotions**
- **Career-defining opportunities**

What's Next?

Now that we've **unlocked the REAL truth about performance reviews**, we're heading into:

Chapter 10: "News Flash, They're Playing Chess, Not Checkers"

- Why corporate success is about strategy, not just talent

- How to think 5 moves ahead in your career

- Mastering long-term positioning so you WIN the game, not just survive it

This one? **The *ultimate* strategy guide for corporate success.**

Chapter 10

News Flash, They're Playing *Chess*, <u>Not</u> Checkers

Corporate Success is About Strategy, Not Just Talent

Let's get straight to it:

Corporate America is a chessboard. If you're playing checkers…making moves without thinking ahead, you are setting yourself up to be **outmaneuvered and overlooked.**

Talent and hard work? Necessary but **not sufficient.**

Strategy, foresight, and calculated moves? That's how you **win.**

The Chessboard: Understanding the Corporate Game

In chess, **every piece has a role**, and **every move has a purpose.** The same applies in corporate environments.

The Pawns: Day-to-Day Tasks

- Pawns represent your **daily responsibilities**.

- They're **essential**, but **focusing solely on them keeps you in the trenches.**

Cheat Code: Excel in your tasks, but **don't get bogged down**. Use them to **position yourself** for bigger moves.

The Knights and Bishops: Lateral and Diagonal Moves

- Knights and bishops symbolize **lateral moves**— taking on projects in **different departments or areas.**

- These moves **expand your skill set** and **increase your visibility**.

Cheat Code: Volunteer for cross-functional teams. Show that you're versatile and can **navigate different terrains.**

The Rooks: Straightforward Power Plays

- **Rooks** move **straight and strong**—they're your **direct promotions** and **leadership** roles.

- To move like a rook, **you need a clear path.**

86

BlackPrint

Cheat Codes for Succeeding in Corporate America as a Black Professional

Cheat Code: Clear obstacles by **building strong relationships** with **key decision-makers**. **Network strategically** to ensure your path is unobstructed.

The Queen: Your Most Powerful Asset

- The queen has the **freedom to move in any direction**—this is **your unique value proposition**.

- It's what **sets you apart** and allows you to **navigate complex situations**.

Cheat Code: **Identify and cultivate your unique strengths.** Leverage them to become **indispensable**.

The King: Your Ultimate Goal

- The **king** represents **your endgame—your ultimate career objectives**.

- **Every move** should be **designed to protect** and **advance** this goal.

Cheat Code: Keep your **end goals in focus**. Ensure that your daily actions and long-term strategies are aligned with where you want to go.

Thinking Five Moves Ahead: Strategic Planning

In chess, success comes from **anticipating your opponent's** moves and **planning accordingly**. In corporate life, this means:

- **Identifying Key Players**

  o **Know who holds power and influence** in your organization.

  o Understand their **motivations, challenges, and goals.**

Cheat Code: Map out the organizational structure. Identify who the decision-makers are and who influences them.

- **Building Alliances**

  o **Forge relationships** with colleagues across all levels.

  o These alliances can provide **support, information, and advocacy.**

Cheat Code: Network both vertically and horizontally. Relationships with peers are just as crucial as those with superiors.

- **Anticipating Challenges**

o **Be aware of potential obstacles**—both systemic and interpersonal.

o Develop **contingency plans** for setbacks.

Cheat Code: Stay informed about company politics and industry trends. This awareness allows you to navigate challenges proactively.

- **Positioning Yourself**

o **Align your personal brand** with the company's mission and values.

o Ensure that **leadership perceives you** as an asset to their goals.

Cheat Code: Regularly communicate your achievements and how they contribute to the organization's success.

- **Making Calculated Risks**

o **Opportunities often require stepping out of your comfort zone.**

o Assess risks, but don't hesitate to make **bold moves** when necessary.

Cheat Code: Weigh the potential benefits against the **risks.** If the upside aligns with your endgame, **take the leap.**

Corporate Cheat Codes: Mastering the Game

Cheat Code #1: Develop a Long-Term Vision

- **Set clear, actionable career goals** for the next 5, 10, and 15 years.

- Use this vision to **guide your decisions and strategies.**

Cheat Code #2: Continuously Upgrade Your Skills

- **Stay ahead by learning new technologies,** methodologies, and industry trends.

- This adaptability makes you valuable and versatile.

Cheat Code #3: Seek Out Mentors and Sponsors

- **Mentors** provide guidance; **sponsors** advocate for you.

- Both are essential for **career advancement.**

Cheat Code #4: Observe and Learn from Others

- **Study the careers of those you admire.**

- Learn from their strategies, mistakes, and successes.

Cheat Code #5: Maintain Your Authenticity

- **Authenticity builds trust and respect.**

- Stay true to your values while navigating the corporate landscape.

Final Thoughts

This chapter is the **culmination of BlackPrint**. It's about recognizing that **corporate success isn't just about playing the game but mastering it** with **strategy, foresight, and authenticity**.

Remember: You're not just a player on the board. With the right moves, you become the **master of the game**.

BlackPrint

Cheat Codes for Succeeding in Corporate America as a Black Professiona

Chapter 11
Navigating Microaggressions
In The Workplace

The Hidden Challenges of Workplace Bias

You've been **there**. You're in a meeting, sharing your ideas, and someone says, **"Wow, you're so articulate."** Or a colleague **assumes you're in a junior role** despite your years of experience. Maybe someone **touches your hair without permission** or **jokes** about how you must have grown up **struggling because you're Black**. These are **microaggressions**—subtle, often unintentional, but **deeply impactful moments of bias** that Black professionals **experience regularly**.

While they may seem small to those delivering them, their **cumulative effect can be exhausting and demoralizing**. **Microaggressions** signal that, **despite your credentials, you are still being othered**—seen as **different**, foreign, or **out of place** in corporate spaces.

This chapter is about recognizing these microaggressions, responding effectively, and shifting the workplace culture toward awareness and accountability.

What Are Microaggressions?

Microaggressions are subtle behaviors, comments, or actions—whether intentional or not—that communicate bias or reinforce stereotypes. They typically fall into three categories:

1. **Micro-assaults:** Overt but indirect discrimination (e.g., "I don't see color" or refusing to acknowledge cultural differences).

2. **Micro-insults:** Subtle but offensive comments (e.g., "You're so well-spoken" or "You don't act Black").

3. **Micro-invalidations:** Dismissing the experiences of marginalized people (e.g., "Racism isn't really an issue here" or "You're overreacting").

Microaggressions aren not just annoying. They create a workplace environment that undermines inclusion, impacts mental health, and can even limit career progression.

The Impact of Microaggressions

Let's be clear—microaggressions are not just minor annoyances. Over time, **they take a real toll on Black professionals,** leading to:

- **Emotional and Mental Exhaustion** – Constantly having to prove yourself or justify your presence can be draining.

- **Self-doubt and Imposter Syndrome** – When your competence is repeatedly questioned, it can erode your confidence.

- **Career Limitations** – Being excluded from conversations, overlooked for promotions, or labeled as "difficult" for addressing bias can stall career growth.

This is why **learning to navigate and challenge microaggressions strategically is critical for Black professionals** in corporate spaces.

How to Respond to Microaggressions

- **Pick Your Battles Strategically**

Not every microaggression requires a full-blown confrontation. Before engaging, consider the context, your emotional bandwidth, and the potential outcome.

Ask yourself:

o Will addressing this educate the person or lead to defensiveness?

o Is this moment worth my energy?

o Can I address this later in a more constructive way?

- **Use the "Call-In" Instead of the "Call-Out" Approach**

Rather than putting someone on the defensive, frame your response in a way that encourages learning.

Example: Instead of, "That's offensive," try: *"I know you may not have meant it this way, but when you said X, it came across as Y."*

"Let's unpack that comment—what do you mean by 'acting Black'?"

This technique forces the person to reflect on their words rather than immediately becoming defensive.

- **Redirect the Conversation**

If a microaggression happens in a meeting or group setting, redirect the discussion to focus on facts and professionalism.

Example: If someone speaks over you or takes credit for your idea:

o *"I'd love to finish my thought on that."*

o *"Yes, that's exactly what I mentioned earlier. Let's build on that."*

- **Keep Receipts**

If you notice a pattern of microaggressions affecting your work or career progression, document them. Keep a record of incidents, dates, and any impact on your role.

- **Leverage Allies and Leadership**

If your workplace has diversity initiatives, affinity groups, or supportive leadership, bring microaggressions to their attention. Sometimes, strategic escalation is necessary.

Holding Organizations Accountable

While individual strategies are essential, the burden should not solely fall on Black professionals to navigate bias. Companies must also take responsibility for:

- **Creating Safe Spaces** – Encouraging open conversations about race, bias, and inclusion.

- **Establishing Reporting Channels** – Ensuring employees can report microaggressions without fear of retaliation.

Real inclusion isn't just about hiring diverse talent—i**t's about fostering a culture where they can thrive without daily obstacles.**

Final Thoughts

Microaggressions may be subtle, but their impact is anything but small. The key to navigating them isn't just enduring—it's responding strategically, protecting your peace, and pushing for cultural change. The goal isn't to "fix" biased colleagues—it's to ensure you are seen, heard, and respected in the corporate space you earned your place in.

What's Next?

Now that we've covered navigating microaggressions, we're diving into another critical topic:

Chapter 12: The Importance of Mental Health and Self-Care

- Recognizing burnout and stress unique to Black professionals

- Developing mental wellness routines that protect your energy

- Seeking support without stigma

Because thriving in corporate America **isn't just about winning**—it's about living and surviving well while doing it.

Let's get into it.

BlackPrint

Cheat Codes for Succeeding in Corporate America as a Black Professional

Chapter 12
The Importance of Mental Health & Self-Care

The Silent Struggle: What Stress Looks Like for *Us*

Black professionals often operate under **constant pressure to excel**, navigating unspoken rules, workplace biases, and higher expectations—all while managing the weight of being **"the only one" in the room.** This unique burden makes **mental health and self-care non-negotiable**, not just for survival but for true **success and fulfillment.**

Let's Talk About:

- The **hidden toll** of corporate stress on Black professionals

- How to **recognize burnout** before it derails you

- **Self-care strategies** that protect your well-being without compromising your ambition

- Why seeking support is not a weakness but a **power move**

The Weight of Being Seen and Unseen

Black professionals often experience dual realities in corporate spaces:

- **You're highly visible,** but your **contributions are overlooked.**

- You're **expected to be resilient** but are **rarely supported.**

- You're **required to be exceptional just to be considered equal.**

This creates a **constant state of stress** that isn't always visible—even to you.

Signs You're Carrying More Than You Realize

Burnout doesn't always show up as exhaustion. Sometimes, it looks like this:

- **Doubting yourself,** even when you **KNOW** you're qualified.

- Feeling **drained by simple interactions** that never used to bother you.

- **Losing patience faster,** especially in meetings where you feel **unheard.**

- **Isolating** yourself from colleagues, friends, and even family.

- **Feeling physically tired**, but your **mind won't slow down.**

If any of this sounds familiar, you're not just tired. You're carrying a mental and emotional load that needs attention.

The Self-Care Shift: Redefining What Rest Looks Like

Most of us were raised to **grind harder, push through, and "rest when the work is done."**

But here's the truth: **The work will NEVER be done.**

If you don't **intentionally protect your mental health,** your **career will take more from you than it gives.**

Three Self-Care Strategies That Work

1. Set Boundaries That Mean Something

- If you're **always the go-to person** at work, you must **start saying no** more often.

- **Stop responding to emails after hours** just to prove you're committed.

- **Take your lunch break.** Block your calendar. **Use your PTO**. Your job is not your life. Protect your time accordingly.

2. Prioritize Rest as a Power Move, Not a Reward

- **Sleep** is a strategic advantage, not a luxury.

- **Breaks increase productivity**—stop guilt-tripping yourself for needing them.

Find ways to unplug mentally:

- **Read a book** for enjoyment, not professional development.

- **Take walks** without your phone.

- **Meditate, journal**, or simply **sit in silence**.

Rest isn't weak—it's a recharge. And, if you keep running on empty, you will crash.

3. Choose Your Energy Wisely

- **Not every battle is worth fighting.** Let some things go.

- **Curate your circle.** If people leave you drained, stop giving them access to you.

- **Protect your peace.** If a situation is **toxic and beyond your control, start planning your exit strategy**—whether that's switching teams, companies, or careers.

The Power of Seeking Support

Therapy, Coaching, and Community: You Don't Have to Do This Alone!

We've been **conditioned to handle everything ourselves.** However, **isolation makes corporate stress more damaging** than it has to be.

Consider these support options:

- **Therapy** – A **trained therapist** can help you process stress, navigate microaggressions, and develop coping mechanisms.

- **Executive Coaching**: A **certified career coach** can help you prepare for leadership, negotiate salaries, and manage workplace challenges.

- **Black Professional Networks** – Join groups where **people understand your experience** and can **provide support and mentorship.**

Asking for help isn't weakness—it's *wisdom.*

Corporate Cheat Codes: Protecting Your Mental Health Like a Boss

Cheat Code #1: Schedule Your Self-Care Like You Schedule Meetings

- **Block time for rest, workouts, hobbies, and unplugging.** Treat them like **non-negotiable appointments.**

Cheat Code #2: Detach Your Worth from Your Work

- You are more than your job title.

- Your value is not tied to productivity.

- Stop seeking validation from a system designed to extract as much as possible from you.

Cheat Code #3: Keep Your Exit Plan Updated

- Every few months, **evaluate: Am I still happy here? Is this still working for me?**

- Keep your resume and network **current, even if you're not job hunting.**

- **Always be ready to pivot—on your terms.**

Final Thoughts

This is the chapter most career books ignore. Because what's the point of climbing the corporate ladder if it's costing you your peace?

- **You don't owe your job your health. You don't owe them burnout.**

- You **owe yourself a career that allows you to thrive, not just survive.**

- **Protect your mental health. Guard your energy. Prioritize your peace.**

That's how you win.

What's Next?

Now that we've **locked in self-care as a career necessity**, we're going into:

Chapter 13: The Exit Strategy—Knowing When to Stay and When to Go

- How to **recognize when a job is no longer serving** you

- **Preparing your next move** before you need it

- How to **leave on your own terms** (with receipts and leverage)

Because staying in a situation that's harming you is not loyalty—it's self-sabotage.

Let's get into it.

Chapter 13
When to Stay
and When to Go

Why This Chapter Matters

Not every job is meant to be forever. Sometimes, the most **brilliant career move** isn't climbing the ladder— it's **knowing when to walk away.**

Whether it's **toxic leadership, stalled growth, or simply a desire for something new,** leaving is a skill, and one that too many Black professionals hesitate to use.

Why?

Because we're often taught to be **grateful** for what we have, to "just **push through**," and to avoid being seen as "job hoppers."

But **staying too long in the wrong place can cost you more than leaving ever will.**

This chapter is about recognizing when it's time to go, preparing your next move strategically, and exiting on your terms—with your reputation, finances, and future intact.

How to Know It's Time to Leave

Should you stay or go? Start by answering these questions:

1. **Is This Job Still Aligned With Your Career Goals?**

   - Am I growing and learning or just existing?

   - Does this job still make sense for where I want to go long-term?

   - Have I hit a ceiling with no path forward?

2. **If you're stagnant, you're falling behind.**

3. **Is the Environment Helping or Hurting You?**

   - You are **consistently overlooked** for promotions.

   - Your work is **undervalued or unrecognized.**

   - The **company has no real commitment to diversity, equity, or inclusion.**

   - You feel **mentally and emotionally drained** more days than not.

- **A bad work environment doesn't have to be abusive to be harmful.**

4. Are You Being Paid What You Deserve?

- Have you checked market rates for your role?

- Do new hires with less experience make more than you?

- Have you been denied raises despite delivering results?

- If **your salary is lagging,** your **company is taking advantage of your loyalty.**

Preparing Your Exit Like a Boss

Leaving isn't just about deciding to go. It's about **setting yourself up** for the **best possible next move.**

1. Get Your Receipts in Order

- **Keep a record of your accomplishments** (metrics, successful projects, wins).

- **Gather written praise from leadership, colleagues,** and **clients.**

111

- **Update your resume and LinkedIn before** announcing your departure.

2. **Your next role should be a step up—and having receipts gives you leverage.**

3. **Start Job Searching BEFORE You Need To**

    - **Tap into your network** and let people know you're open to new opportunities.

    - Target **companies with cultures and values** that **align with what you need**.

    - **Brush up on your interview skills**—because you're about to be in high demand.

4. **Negotiate Everything**

    - **Salary & Bonuses** – Ensure you're paid at or above market value.

    - **Title & Responsibilities** – Get clarity on expectations before signing.

    - **Remote & Flexibility** – If it matters to you, make it a condition.

    - **Professional Development** – Request a budget for conferences, courses, or certifications.

- You're not just taking a job. You're setting the foundation for your future.

Making a Strong Exit

When it's time to go, leave on a high note.

1. **Give Proper Notice (But Not Too Much)**

   - **Two weeks is standard, but read the room.** If your role is critical, consider giving a more extended notice (**but only if it benefits YOU**).

   - **Be prepared to leave immediately.** Some companies cut access the moment you resign.

2. **Stay Professional (Even If They Don't Deserve It)**

   - **No exit interviews that turn into therapy sessions.** Keep it brief and neutral.

   - **No burning bridges.** Even if you hated it there, industries are small, and reputations travel.

   - No trash-talking on social media. Protect your brand at all costs.

3. **Leave With Relationships, Not Just Regrets**

- **Connect with mentors, colleagues, and allies** before leaving.

- **Send a thoughtful farewell email** (focused on gratitude, not grievances).

- **Keep the doors open** for future collaborations and opportunities.

Corporate Cheat Codes: Leaving Like a Boss

Cheat Code #1: Always Be Ready to Walk

- **Stay connected** to recruiters and industry leaders.

- **Never get too comfortable** in a job that isn't serving you.

Cheat Code #2: Protect Your Reputation

- **How you leave matters** as much as how you stay.

- **Exit with professionalism and strategy,** even if the company wasn't great to you.

- **People remember** your last impression. Make it count.

Cheat Code #3: Never Accept Less Than You Deserve

- Know your **worth.**

- Negotiate **without fear.**

- Move with **confidence.**

Final Thoughts

Most people avoid this part of career growth, but mastering the exit is as important as mastering the climb.

You don't owe any company your loyalty at the expense of your own success. When it's time to go, **leave on your terms,** with your **head high and your next move already lined up.**

BlackPrint

Cheat Codes for Succeeding in Corporate America as a Black Professional

Chapter 14
Long-Term Career Strategies

Success is a Marathon, Not a Sprint

The goal is not just to survive corporate America—it's to thrive, create impact, and build a career. This requires **long-term strategic thinking**, not just focusing on the next promotion or paycheck.

Too many Black professionals spend their careers in "survival mode," **navigating obstacles but never truly positioning themselves for long-term success.**

This chapter is about stepping back, looking at the big picture, and making intentional moves that set you up for sustained success, influence, and generational impact.

The Five Pillars of a Legacy-Building Career

There's a **difference between working a job and building a career that outlasts you**. Here's how you ensure that your career moves create **lasting value**:

1. Define Your Endgame—What's Your Ultimate Goal?

A **strong career strategy starts with clarity on where you want to end up.** If you don't have a long-term goal, you'll keep making short-term decisions that don't serve your future.

Key Questions to Ask Yourself:

* Where do I want to be in 5, 10, or 20 years?

* Do I want to be a **C-suite executive, an entrepreneur,** an **industry thought leader**, or something else?

* What kind of **impact do I want to have on the next generation** of Black professionals?

Once you identify your endgame, every move you make should align with that vision.

Action Step: Write down your long-term career goal and identify three key milestones you need to hit to get there.

2. Play the Long Game—Make Moves That Matter

Short-term wins feel good, but long-term plays win the game. Don't just chase titles—chase opportunities that build the skills, experiences, and networks you need for sustained success.

Strategic Moves to Consider:

- **Seek Stretch Roles:** Take on **challenging assignments, expose yourself** to **decision-makers,** and expand your influence.

- **Build a High-Value Network: Connect with executives, mentors, and sponsors** who can open doors and advocate for your growth.

- **Own Your Narrative: Control how you're perceived in your industry** by consistently delivering excellence and showcasing your impact.

Action Step: Identify one strategic move you can make this year to bring you closer to your long-term goal.

3. Invest in Your Brand—Make Your Name Carry Weight

Your name should **mean something** in your industry.

People should associate you with **excellence, leadership, and innovation.** That doesn't happen by accident—**it happens by design.**

Ways to Strengthen Your Brand:

- **Become a Thought Leader: Speak at conferences, write articles,** and **share insights** that position you as an expert.

- **Master Public Speaking: Strong communicators rise faster in leadership.** Invest in your speaking skills to build executive presence.

- **Showcase Your Work:** Don't just do great work— **make sure people see it.** Keep a record of your achievements and share them strategically.

Action Step: Develop a plan to **enhance your personal brand** over the next year. Focus on one of the above areas first.

4. Pay It Forward—Lift as You Climb

Your success isn't just about you—it's about **creating opportunities** for **others.** Black professionals who reach leadership levels have a **responsibility to mentor, sponsor, and uplift the next generation.**

Ways to Give Back While Advancing:

- **Mentor Upcoming Talent:** Share the lessons you've learned with younger professionals.

- **Advocate for Diverse Hiring & Promotion Practices:** Use your influence to push for systemic change within your company.

- **Support Black-Owned Businesses & Networks:** Build economic power by investing in Black professionals and entrepreneurs.

Action Step: Identify one way to support another Black professional's growth this year.

5. Build Wealth, Not Just a Paycheck

A high salary doesn't equal financial freedom. True success includes financial stability and generational wealth.

Many Black professionals get stuck in cycles of **high earning but low wealth-building** due to systemic barriers and lack of financial literacy.

Wealth-Building Strategies:

- **Invest Early & Consistently:** Maximize retirement accounts, stocks, and real estate investments.

- **Negotiate Salary & Equity:** Never accept the first offer—advocate for your worth.

- **Diversify Income Streams:** Build multiple revenue sources so you're not solely dependent on a corporate paycheck.

Action Step: Take one financial step this year, such as increasing your savings, investing, or seeking financial advice.

Final Thoughts: Own Your Career Like a CEO

Corporate success isn't just about working hard—it's about working smart, positioning yourself strategically, and making moves that build power, influence, and impact. As you move forward, remember:

- **Be intentional.** Every decision should bring you closer to your endgame.

- **Be visible.** Don't let your talent go unnoticed—position yourself where it counts.

- **Be fearless. You belong in every room you step into.** Walk in like you **own it.**

This is more than a career—it's a legacy in the making. Build it.

What's Next?

With a legacy-building mindset, you're now ready to master the final and most critical chapter:

Chapter 15: Leaving a Legacy

We'll explore:

- Shifting from personal success to collective progress

- Why Legacy Matters

- Using your influence to make lasting changes

Let's get into it.

BlackPrint

Cheat Codes for Succeeding in Corporate America as a Black Professional

Chapter 15
Leaving a Legacy

Success Isn't Just About You—It's About Who You Lift Up

By now, you've mastered the strategies, the politics, and the power moves necessary to navigate corporate America.

But **real success isn't just about personal achievement,** it's about creating a path for others to follow. **It's about** *legacy.*

A legacy is more than a title, a salary, or a corner office. It's **the impact you leave behind, the doors you open for others, and the change you help create.**

If you've **worked this hard to break barriers,** why not **ensure that others don't have to work twice as hard to do the same?**

This chapter is about **shifting from personal success to collective progress**—making sure that as you rise, you **lift others with you.**

Why Legacy Matters

Corporate America was not designed for us, but we are here anyway—**breaking ceilings, challenging norms, and proving our excellence.**

But if **every generation** of **Black professionals** has to **start from scratch, the struggle never end**s.

Legacy means ensuring that the lessons you've learned, the wins you've fought for, and the battles you've won don't die with you.

It's about:

- **Creating pathways** for future Black professionals so they don't face the same obstacles you did.

- **Sharing knowledge** so others don't have to learn the hard way.

- **Using your influence** to make lasting changes in corporate culture, policy, and opportunity.

How to Build a Legacy in Corporate America

Leaving an impact isn't just about what you achieve—it's about **what you leave behind for others**. Here's how you can ensure that your success outlives you:

1. Be a Sponsor, Not Just a Mentor

- Mentorship is valuable, but sponsorship is game-changing. If you genuinely want to **create opportunities** for the next generation, **don't just offer advice—offer access.**

- **Advocate** for Black talent in **leadership meetings.**

- **Recommend high-potential** professionals for **significant projects.**

- **Use your influence** to **open doors** that others might not even know exist.

A sponsor doesn't just guide you—they fight for you. Be that person for someone else.

2. Leave Institutional Knowledge Behind

Too often, Black professionals learn valuable corporate survival skills only through trial and error. Don't let that knowledge disappear when you move on.

- **Create guides, playbooks, or internal resources** to help Black employees navigate challenges.

- **Host lunch-and-learns** to share career acceleration strategies.

- **Form employee resource groups** (ERGs) that provide ongoing support and mentorship.

3. Create Sustainable Change in Your Organization

True legacy isn't just about individual wins—it's about shifting systems.

- **Advocate for fair hiring practices** that bring in more Black talent.

- **Push for pay equity and transparency** to close racial wage gaps.

- **Hold leadership accountable** for genuine **inclusion efforts,** not just performative gestures.

If policies and structures don't change, progress is temporary. Legacy builders make sure progress lasts.

4. Normalize Black Leadership

One of the **most powerful ways to create lasting impact is simply by existing in spaces where we were never meant to be**—and **making sure we aren't the last.**

- Be **visible and vocal** as a leader.

- **Share your journey** so others see that it's possible.

- **Build a network** of Black professionals so that no one moves alone.

When Black leadership becomes the norm rather than the exception, we redefine what's possible for future generations.

5. Pay It Forward

Success is best when it's shared. Whatever level you've reached, pull others up with you.

- **Offer free coaching or career guidance** to younger professionals.

- **Invest in Black-owned businesses** and initiatives.

- **Donate to scholarships, nonprofits, and programs that uplift Black talent.**

Legacy isn't just about what you build—it's about what you give back.

Corporate Cheat Codes: Securing Your Legacy

Cheat Code #1: Document Your Knowledge

- **Write down** the strategies, insights, and lessons that helped you succeed.

- **Share them with younger professionals** or create a leadership guide.

Cheat Code #2: Speak Up for Others When They're Not in the Room

- If a talented Black employee isn't being recognized, **say their name.**

- **Use your credibility** to push for their advancement.

Cheat Code #3: Create a Lasting Impact Beyond Your Job

- Whether through policy changes, mentorship programs, or financial support, **make sure your influence extends beyond your tenure.**

Final Thoughts

This is about **making sure that all the hard work you've put into mastering corporate America doesn't end with you.** It's about **shifting from individual success to collective empowerment.**

Success is great—but legacy is greater.

Because when Black professionals move forward together, **we don't just play the game—we change it.**

What's Next?

With BlackPrint complete, it's time to:

- **Implement these strategies** in your daily professional life.

- **Share this knowledge** with others to empower our community.

- **Continue evolving, learning, and positioning** yourself for greatness.

The game is ours to master. **LET'S PLAY TO WIN.**

BlackPrint

Cheat Codes for Succeeding in Corporate America as a Black Professional

References Supporting Key Concepts in *BlackPrint*

Corporate Dynamics and Workplace Biases

Pew Research Center (2023). *Black workers' views and experiences in the U.S. labor force.* – Finds that 41% of Black employees have experienced discrimination in hiring, pay, or promotions because of their race (versus only 8% of White workers) (Pewresearch.org). About half of Black workers also feel that being Black makes it harder to succeed at their workplace (Pewresearch.rog), underscoring persistent bias in corporate environments.

Harvard Business School – Working Knowledge (2023). *Black Employees Not Only Earn Less, But Deal with Bad Bosses and Poor Conditions.* – Highlights that Black workers not only face a 30–35% pay gap but are also less likely to have supportive managers or positive work cultures (Library.HBS.edu). This research shows that Black employees disproportionately endure poorer workplace conditions (e.g., unsupportive bosses and weaker work-life balance) in addition to pay inequities (Library.HBS.edu).

BlackPrint

Cheat Codes for Succeeding in Corporate America as a Black Professional

LeanIn & McKinsey (2020). *The State of Black Women in Corporate America.* – Reveals that 49% of Black women feel their race will make it harder to get a raise or promotion, compared to just 3% of White women (LEANIN.ORG). It also notes a "broken rung" in promotions – for every 100 men promoted to manager, only 58 Black women are promoted (LEANIN.ORG) – highlighting structural barriers and biases Black professionals face in climbing corporate ranks.

Leadership Strategies for Black Professionals

Korn Ferry & ELC (2019). *The Black P&L Leader Study.* – Found that 60% of senior Black executives "would never leave their career decisions to chance," instead taking a highly strategic, analytical approach to managing their careers (KornFerry.com). Over 80% were willing to embrace greater risks and seek out tough assignments to gain influence, and nearly 60% felt they had to work twice as hard as peers to prove their worth (KornFerry.com). These insights underline the proactive planning, extra effort, and calculated risk-taking that Black leaders employ to advance.

NACE (2022). *Understanding How Black Women Navigate Their Careers.* – A study identified four key "career assets" for Black women's professional growth: mentorship, community support, bicultural competence, and resilience (Naceweb.org). In practice, this meant building supportive networks, learning to operate across different cultural environments, and persevering through challenges – strategies that help Black professionals develop as leaders and overcome workplace obstacles.

Korn Ferry (2021). *Blacks in Leadership: Harder Than It Should Have Been.* – Reports that more than half of Black executives felt they had to take much bigger risks than other leaders in order to advance (e.g. stepping into high-stakes roles) and often faced higher performance standards (KornFerry.com) (KornFerry.com). Many also spoke of actively seeking out P&L roles and critical projects to showcase their abilities, reflecting a deliberate strategy to position themselves for leadership opportunities.

Sponsorship vs. Mentorship

McKinsey (2021). *Race in the Workplace: The Black Experience in the US Private Sector.* – Highlights that roughly two-thirds of Black employees (and employees overall) report having **no sponsor** at work (MCKINSEY.COM) (MCKINSEY.COM). Despite many companies offering mentoring, a lack of true sponsorship (senior leaders advocating for talent) is a key gap holding Black professionals back. The study links this sponsorship void to slower promotion rates for Black employees, even as companies voice commitments to diversity.

Sylvia Ann Hewlett – Center for Talent Innovation (2013). *Forget a Mentor, Find a Sponsor.* – Demonstrates the outsized impact of sponsorship on career progression. For Black professionals in particular, having a sponsor yields dramatic benefits: an African-American manager with a sponsor is 51% more likely to advance to a higher level ( ). Moreover, Black employees with sponsors are far more likely to stay with their companies (over twice as likely in one study) (SylviaAnnHewlett.com), showing that sponsorship not only fuels advancement but also improves retention.

Korn Ferry & ELC (2019). *The Black P&L Leader Study.* – Underscores that mentorship alone is not enough – **81%** of Black P&L executives said having a sponsor was *indispensable* to their career progression (KornFerry.com). These senior leaders credit sponsors with providing exposure to opportunities and actively advocating for them, whereas mentors provided advice. The finding reinforces the book's point that a sponsor's advocacy is a "cheat code" for breaking through glass ceilings that many Black professionals otherwise hit (INSIDEINDIANABUSINESS.COM).

Executive Presence and Perception Management

SHRM/Forbes (2022). *"Black Employees Are Penalized for Self-Promotion, Study Finds"* Discusses new research showing that when Black employees engage in self-promotion (a common tactic to get noticed for advancement), it can backfire due to bias. Black employees who touted their accomplishments were rated **less favorably** on performance and fit compared to White, Asian, or Hispanic colleagues (SHRM.ORG). This suggests Black professionals must be more cautious and deliberate in managing how they project confidence and highlight achievements, to avoid negative perceptions.

Korn Ferry & ELC (2019). *The Black P&L Leader Study.* – Reveals that nearly 60% of Black executives felt they had to **"work twice as hard to accomplish twice as much"** as their peers just to counteract stereotypes and misperceptions about their capabilities (KORNFERRY.COM). In practice, many described constantly having to prove themselves to be seen as equally competent. This finding illustrates the extra burden on Black professionals to curate an impeccable image and performance record – essentially, an ongoing perception management strategy to earn the same recognition as others.

Harvard Business Review (2019). *"The Costs of Code-Switching."* – Explores how Black professionals often adjust their language, demeanor, or appearance in the workplace to conform to majority norms and put others at ease. This "code-switching" is described as altering one's speech, behavior, or self-expression **to optimize the comfort of others in exchange for fair treatment and opportunities** (LSA.UMICH.EDU). While adopting a different persona at work can help Black employees navigate corporate culture and demonstrate "executive presence" in a traditional sense, the article notes it comes at a psychological cost and can impede authenticity (LSA.UMICH.EDU) (LSA.UMICH.EDU). It underlines the complex balance Black professionals must manage between authenticity and fitting the expected leadership mold.

Performance Reviews and Corporate Politics

Harvard Kennedy School (2021). *The Role of Gender and Race in Performance Appraisals.* – A data analysis of a global company's evaluations found clear racial bias in performance reviews. Managers tended to give employees of color significantly lower ratings than those employees gave themselves, even **after** seeing the self-evaluations (HKS.HARVARD.EDU). By contrast, managers boosted the scores of White women to correct for their lower self-ratings. This suggests that Black and other minority employees are held to tougher scrutiny in reviews, which can hinder promotions and pay – a reality that confirms the need to navigate office politics and biases expertly.

LeanIn/McKinsey (2017). *Women in the Workplace – Women of Color Findings.* – Reported that only **23%** of Black women said their managers helped them navigate organizational politics, and just 28% felt their managers advocated for them or defended their work (HERAGENDA.COM). Black professionals often lack the behind-the-scenes support that others receive in understanding unwritten rules or having their backs in meetings. This absence of political support means they must often figure out corporate dynamics alone and can be disadvantaged in performance calibration discussions.

Pew Research Center (2023). *Racial Bias in Hiring and Performance Evaluations.* – In a national survey, 56% of Black adults said that bias based on race is a **major problem** in how performance evaluations are conducted in companies (PEWRESEARCH.ORG). By contrast, only 23% of White adults viewed bias in performance reviews as a major issue (PEWRESEARCH.ORG). This perception gap highlights the lived experience of Black employees with evaluation processes that may undervalue their contributions. It reinforces the importance of vigilance and strategy when undergoing reviews and underscores why Black professionals often put extra effort into office politics – to ensure fair evaluation and advancement.

Career Advancement Strategies and Long-Term Positioning

Korn Ferry & ELC (2019). *The Black P&L Leader Study.* – Emphasizes the value of long-term career strategy. 60% of Black executives interviewed said they charted their careers very deliberately, taking charge of their own advancement rather than waiting passively for opportunities (KORNFERRY.COM). Many cultivated diverse experiences – for instance, **50%** purposely sought out especially challenging projects with profit-and-loss responsibility to gain skills and visibility early in their careers (KORNFERRY.COM). This proactive, strategic positioning (rotating through stretch roles and building a track record) helped set them up for senior leadership over time.

Energy Capital & Power (2023). *Creating Pathways to Success: Strategies for Black Professionals.* – A recent industry insight piece that outlines practical long-term career strategies. It advises Black professionals to **set clear goals, build robust networks, continuously develop skills, and actively promote their personal brand** to advance in corporate environments (Energycapitalpower.com)

(ENERGYCAPITALPOWER.COM). By networking within and beyond their organizations (including finding mentors/sponsors), expanding their expertise, and showcasing their achievements, Black employees can better position themselves for future opportunities and leadership roles.

Management Leadership for Tomorrow (2023). *Retention of High-Performing People of Color.* – Notes that 55% of surveyed high-achieving professionals of color do not plan to stay at their current company for more than two years (MLT.ORG). The main reasons were a lack of belonging and lack of confidence in their growth path. This finding, though about retention, highlights a key career strategy: Black professionals often must think several moves ahead. Many proactively switch organizations or roles to attain advancement when they see limited growth internally. Long-term success thus may involve being willing to pursue new opportunities at other companies or negotiating for clearer advancement plans, rather than remaining stagnant in one role or company.

About the Author

Strategist. Leader. Change-Maker.

Monique L. Thompson

A Certified Executive, Leadership, and Professional Coach and Certified Myers-Briggs Practitioner, Monique specializes in breaking barriers, securing leadership roles, and redefining career trajectories. As a published author, international speaker, and equity advocate, she is committed to ensuring Black professionals don't just get a seat at the table—they know how to use it.

Monique is the author of **three transformational books**:

BlackPrint (this book): Cheat Codes for How to Succeed in Corporate America as a Black Professional: A no-nonsense, strategy-packed guide to navigating power, positioning for success, and executing with intention.

143

BlackPrint

Cheat Codes for Succeeding in Corporate America as a Black Professional

The Ladder Has Rungs: A bold and eye-opening look at how women navigate modern dating, relationships, and the male relationship paradigm. This book helps `women understand their worth, power, and choices in love and partnership.

BeeCause You Loved Me: A heartfelt and compelling exploration of resilience, healing, and the transformative power of unconditional love.

Ready to take your career or your personal growth to the next level?

Visit **www.moniquelthompson.com** to connect with Monique for executive coaching, leadership training, or speaking engagements.

Connect with Monique on social media:
@iammothompson

www.BlackPrintSuccess.com

www.ingramcontent.com/pod-product-compliance
Lightning Source LLC
Chambersburg PA
CBHW072152270326
41930CB00011B/2402